T0065490

SAYETH
THE LORD

LEESE E. I. FORD

BELIEVER OF JESUS (NOT LUCK)
SERVANT OF GOD

WESTBOW
PRESS®
A DIVISION OF THOMAS NELSON
& ZONDERVAN

Copyright © 2021 Leese E. I. Ford.

All rights reserved. No part of this book may be used or reproduced by
any means, graphic, electronic, or mechanical, including photocopying,
recording, taping or by any information storage retrieval system
without the written permission of the author except in the case of
brief quotations embodied in critical articles and reviews.

WestBow Press books may be ordered through booksellers or by contacting:

WestBow Press
A Division of Thomas Nelson & Zondervan
1663 Liberty Drive
Bloomington, IN 47403
www.westbowpress.com
844-714-3454

Because of the dynamic nature of the Internet, any web addresses or
links contained in this book may have changed since publication and
may no longer be valid. The views expressed in this work are solely those
of the author and do not necessarily reflect the views of the publisher,
and the publisher hereby disclaims any responsibility for them.

Any people depicted in stock imagery provided by Getty Images are
models, and such images are being used for illustrative purposes only.
Certain stock imagery © Getty Images.

Unless otherwise noted, scripture quotations marked are taken from the Holy
Bible, New International Version®, NIV®. Copyright © 1973, 1978, 1984, 2011 by
Biblica, Inc.™ Used by permission of Zondervan. All rights reserved worldwide.
www.zondervan.com The "NIV" and "New International Version" are trademarks
registered in the United States Patent and Trademark Office by Biblica, Inc.™

Scripture marked (KJV) taken from the King James Version of the Bible.

ISBN: 978-1-6642-2406-3 (sc)
ISBN: 978-1-6642-2405-6 (e)

Print information available on the last page.

WestBow Press rev. date: 3/15/2021

WELCOME!!!

HIS MESSAGE MINISTRY

H.M.M.-Something to Think about!!!

Get in Touch with THE LORD!!!

Thank you for visiting
(http://www.HisMessageMinistry.com)

Where it's always a Good Time to Spread The Word!!!
We thank you for your support, which
helps others to know Jesus!!!

This page is dedicated to those who have helped tremendously in the publishing of this book. I greatly appreciate all the work you have done to help me.

GOD - For giving me Life and my Ministry
Jessie, Raymond, and William James
Kate - My first life-long best friend
Mom - Inspirational
Richard - For your unfailing understanding
Sha and Amy - <u>BFsF</u>
David S. - For being an Inspiration
Angie and Sheena - You Inspire,
Empower, and Encourage me
Bob A. - Thanks for The Second
Chance and Encouragement
Donovan – For reminding me of who I am in Christ
Eugene - For being there for me
Mrs. Janet - My Spiritual Mentor
Mrs. Clara - For the Wisdom you depart
John S. - In depth Thoughts
Ryan V. - Empowering Motivator
Brennon N. - Being a big Brother

Family and Friends from Blue Jean Selma, Crosspoint and Christ The King who have made a lasting impression on me and all the employees at Selma-Dallas County Public Library and more...

I Love you all.

MY TESTIMONY

I came from a broken home. I was in foster care at a young age. From there, I grew up to be a young mother.

At seventeen, I was an alcoholic. Probably the same year, I was well on my way to being addicted to drugs. I went through relationship after relationship. I would keep them for 4-5 years, then just leave.

My addiction took me down suicide paths; sexual, physical, and mental abuse. My second Driving Under the Influence (D. U. I.) landed me in front of the same Judge as my first D. U. I.. I was ready for a Change. I couldn't handle my own Life anymore. I wanted a Change that would be permanent and lasting. I was so tired of chasing the money, to chase the drug, to chase the money for more gas and more drugs. I had to give my life up to realize that I couldn't make it without Christ. I knew I had to give up my agenda and Trust Him to take care of me.

Phil. 4:19 NIV
And my GOD will meet all your needs according
to the riches of His Glory in Christ Jesus.
GOD redeemed me, and He can redeem you, too.

Read Romans 10:9-10(NIV)
We thank you for your support of our Ministry. If you have any questions, please feel free to call us at 1-844-SEEK-HIM (1-844-7335-446), or write us at:

His Message Ministry
P. O. Box 1122
Selma, Al. 36702

BIBLE VERSES ON ANGER

Romans 1:18-19 NIV
The wrath of GOD is being revealed from Heaven
against all the godlessness and wickedness of people,
who suppress the truth by their wickedness, since
what may be known about GOD is plain to them,
because GOD has made it plain to them.

Ephesians 4:26-27 NIV
In your anger do not sin: do not let the sun go down while
you are still angry, and do not give the devil a foothold.

James l: 19-21 NIV
My dear Brothers and Sisters, take note of this: Everyone
should be quick to listen, slow to speak and slow to
become angry, because human anger does not produce the
righteousness that GOD desires. Therefore, get rid of all
moral filth and the evil that is so prevalent and humbly
accept The Word planted in you, which can save you.

Proverbs 29:11 NIV
Fools give full vent to their rage, but
the wise bring calm in the end.

Proverbs 19:11 NIV

A person's wisdom yields patience; it is to
one's glory to overlook an offense.

Ecclesiastes 7:9 NIV
Do not be quickly provoked in your spirit,
for anger resides in the lap of fools.

Proverbs 15:1 NIV
A gentle answer turns away wrath, but
a harsh word stirs up anger.

Proverbs 15:18 NIV
A hot-tempered man stirs up dissention,
but a patient man calms a quarrel.

Colossians 3:8 and Eph. 4:31 NIV
But now you must rid yourself of all things as these: anger,
rage, malice, slander, and filthy language from your lips.

Proverbs 22:24 NIV
Do not make friends with a hot-tempered man,
do not associate with one easily angered.

Proverbs 14:29 NIV
A patient man has great understanding, but
a quick-tempered man displays folly.

Proverbs 16:32 NIV
Better a patient man than a warrior, a man who
controls his temper than one who takes a city

CONTENTS

Please be sure to read all Bible verses from your Bible.
These Bible verses are NIV; unless specified otherwise.

Thank you and have a Blessed day; (DAILY)!!!

SAYETH THE LORD

May 23, 2014

These things THE LORD did say this morning:

GOD always judges by Heart and Faith: forgiving anything that we have done in the past (as long as we asked for forgiveness and have repented). All is washed anew. We, who are in Christ, have been Called to Walk with THE LORD. Hold Strong to The Promise that I (THE LORD, your GOD) gave you- Blessings are yet to come. Hold true to The Truth you KNOW about Me. Stand firm in your Faith. Worship Me more, so you will KNOW Me more. I have run the darkness out of your Life. Let your Light shine. I will always shine a Light to guide your feet along My Path. I will put those in your path who need to hear from Me. Just listen for what I tell you. The ones who don't get Healed this time, keep Praying, be Strong, for your Prayers are being Heard. Keep being My Light! For every time you Minister to someone, they see My Light shining through you. Blessed are those who Hear.

Carry My Message to others - today and forever!!!

SAYETH THE LORD

— 1 —

ENCOURAGEMENT

Draw near to GOD and He will draw near to you.
James 4:8 NIV
GOD is my: (NIV)
Father...Isaiah 9:6
Love... 1 John 4:16
Salvation.... John 3:3; John 3:16; Romans 10:9
Eternal Life... 1 John 5:20
Peace... 2 Thessalonians 3:1-6
Counselor... Proverbs 20:22
Shield... Psalms 144:2; Joel 3:16
Wisdom... James 1:5
Hiding Place... Psalms 32:7
Resting Place... Jeremiah 6:16; Psalms 62:1
Redeemer... Isaiah 59:20
Deliverer... Psalms 70:5
Helper... Hebrews 13:6
Healer... Psalm 103:3
Hope... Psalms 71:5
Strength... Psalm -43:2
Friend... John 15:15
Restorer... Psalm 23:3
Provider... Genesis 22:14
Truth... John 16:13
<u>THE LORD'S PRAYER</u>
<u>MATTHEW 6:9-15</u>

HELP IN TIME
OF NEED

(NIV)
The Way of Salvation
John 3:3; John 3:16; Romans 10:9

PEACE in Time of Anxiety:
Psalms 4; Philippians 4:6-7; Matthew 6:25-34; John 14

COURAGE in Time of Fear:
Psalms 46; Hebrews 13:5-6; 2 Corinthians 4:8-18

RELIEF in Time of Suffering:
Psalms 41; Psalms 91; 2 Corinthians 12:8-
10; and Hebrews 12:3-13; Ephesians 1:3

GUIDANCE in Time of Decision:
Psalms 32; James 1:5-6; Hebrews 4:16; Genesis 50:15-21

COMFORT in Time of Sorrow:
Philippians 4:13; Psalms 43; 2 Corinthians
1:3-5; Romans 8:26-28

<u>REJOICING in Time of Forgiveness:</u>
Psalms 51; John 3:16-17; 1 John 4:7-10

<u>THE LORD'S PRAYER:</u>
<u>Matthew 6:9-15</u>
Make and go over your list of GOD'S Blessings!

ARMOR OF GOD

Ephesians 6:10-18 NIV

Finally, be strong in THE LORD and in His Mighty Power. Put on the full Armor of God, so that you can take your stand against the devil's schemes. For our struggle is not against flesh and blood, but against the rulers, against authorities, against the powers of this dark world and against the spiritual forces of evil in The Heavenly Realms.

Therefore, put on the full Armor of God, so that when the day of evil comes, you may be able to stand your ground, and after you have done everything, to stand.

Stand firm then, with The Belt of Truth buckled around your waist, with The Breastplate of Righteousness in place, and with your feet fitted with the readiness that comes from the Gospel of Peace. In addition to all this, take up The Shield of Faith, with which you can extinguish all the flaming arrows of the evil one. Take The Helmet of Salvation and The Sword of The Spirit, which is The Word of God.

And Pray in The Spirit on all occasions with all kinds of Prayers and requests. With this in mind, be alert and always keep on Praying for all The Lord's people.

Be strong and of good cheer, for The Lord is with you at all Times. He has made a promise to never leave us, nor forsake us. Be Blessed today knowing that God Loves you!!!

Put on your Armor of God and let's go fight this fight!!!

In Jesus' Holy Name, we Pray!!! A-MEN!!!

A SURVIVAL KIT
FOR EVERYDAY!!!

<u>TOOTHPICK</u>
To remind you to pick out the good qualities in others!
Matthew 7:1 NIV

<u>RUBBER BAND</u>
To remind you to be flexible, things might not
always go the way you want, but it will work out!
Romans 8:28 NIV

<u>BAND-AID</u>
To remind you to Heal hurt feelings, yours or someone else's.
Col. 3:12-14 NIV

<u>PENCIL</u>
To remind you to list your Blessings everyday.
Ephesians 1:3 NIV

<u>ERASER</u>
To remind you that everyone makes mistakes, and it's okay.
Genesis 50:15-21 NIV

CHEWING GUM
To remind you to stick with it and you can
accomplish anything with Jesus.
Philippians 4:13 NIV

MINT
To remind you that you are worth a
mint to your Heavenly Father.
John 3:6-17 NIV

CANDY KISS
To remind you that: John 3:16 NIV

This is GOD'S Gift to you. Use it well
and may GOD richly Bless you!!!

BATTLING DISCOURAGEMENT!!!

(All are NIV)

Hope is the catalyst of your future.

Thank You, Jesus, for being by my side and KNOWING what I need, when I need it, before I need it!!!

People give up, quit Walking with The Lord and have fear. They are angry, frustrated, withdrawn, and have negativities. These are the people who have false beliefs-such as --- "For luck.". THERE IS NO SUCH THING AS LUCK.

<u>IT'S ALL BY THE GRACE OF GOD!!!</u>

We carry Joy, Peace, Love, Positivity (Faith, Hope and Love), -the greatest of these being Love.

Romans 8:28 READS:

And we know that in ALL things GOD works for the good of those who Love Him, who have been called according to His Purpose.

1 Timothy 6:17 READS:

Command those who are rich in this present world not to be arrogant nor to put their Hope in wealth, which is so uncertain, but to put their Hope in GOD, who richly provides us with everything for our enjoyment.

Put your Hope in GOD, not in your own ability. Get focused securely back on GOD, and all Hope will return. Hebrews 6:17-20; 1 Thess. 5:ALL.

IN JESUS' HOLY NAME, we PRAY!!! A-MEN!!

SERENITY PRAYER

GOD grant me the SERENITY to accept the things I cannot change,
COURAGE to change the things I can,
and the WISDOM to KNOW the difference.
Living one day at a Time,
enjoying one moment at a Time,
accepting hardship as a pathway to Peace;
taking as Jesus did, this sinful world as it is,
not as I would have it; trusting that You will all things right
if I surrender to Your Will; so that I may be reasonably happy
in this Life and supremely happy with You forever in the next.

A-MEN!!!
Reinhold Niebuhr

TREASURE EVERY MOMENT

Treasure every moment that you have today, always treasuring the moments more because you were able to share them with someone special.

For <u>this moment</u> is special enough for you to take time out of your busy day to spend it with your Loved ones.

Remember this always, <u>TIME WAITS FOR NO ONE</u>!

Yesterday is history, tomorrow is a mystery, but today is a precious Gift from GOD!!!

That's why it is called the Present!

Thank GOD we are able to share these Precious Moments of Time with our Loved ones!!!

WHEN YOU'RE BLESSED ABUNDANCE!!!

(All are NIV)

Read: 2 Corinthians 9:6-15; Gal. 6:6-8; Proverbs 14:14-16

What you plant is what you get. If you plant few seeds, you harvest few crops. Also if you are planting bad seeds, (showing criminal behavior), then jail and court you shall receive. If showing Grace, Mercy and Forgiveness is what you do, then you will store up Heavenly Treasures.

Show Grace, Mercy, and Forgiveness in all you do, because GOD forgave us our sins when He sent His Only Son to die on The Cross for OUR sins. THE LORD Jesus had no sin.

Give honestly and truly from the heart with much happiness. Give freely and it shall be returned ten-fold. Live in The Overflow of Blessings yet unseen. (The Blessings are just not here yet.)

Live abundantly, speak Blessings over each other and BE Holy in all you do, for THE LORD Knows all things.

In Jesus' Holy, Heavenly Name, we Pray!!! A-MEN!!!

TIME IS RUNNING OUT!!!

11-20-13

I was on a slippery (muddy) slope, being drawn toward the pit. I had no chains or ropes drawing or pushing me. A big white clock (that I couldn't see) lay at the bottom of the pit in front of me, ticking away, loudly and waiting. I look up and see a sand clock (up above me and to the RIGHT).

I study closer and the sand clock is draining, first slowly, then faster and faster, always leaving a little sand in the clock. Behind this pit, I see a Death Cloud.

THE MEANING OF THIS DREAM IS:

TIME IS RUNNING OUT!!! CHOOSE YE NOW!!!

I hesitated at death's door. I didn't want to die. The dream is ALL about our time (HERE on earth). It is only a short time. We are all free to choose between Heaven and Hell. If you died today, where would you go?

John 3:16: (KJV)

For GOD so loved the world that He gave His one and only Son, that whoever believes in Him shall not perish but have Eternal Life.

Don't forget GOD and where He has brought you from and The Blessings yet to come.

THE WAY OF THE CROSS IS THE WAY HOME. If any of you wish to have THE LORD Jesus Christ as your Savior: Please Pray with me: Dear LORD: I have done wrong in Your Eyes. Thank You for dying (for my sins) on the Cross. I accept You as my LORD AND SAVIOR. Let me humbly Serve You.

IN JESUS' NAME WE PRAY!!! A-MEN!!!

THE IMPORTANCE
OF GOD'S PRESENCE

3-4-2014

We always wonder in moments of quiet, (when we are down) if GOD is with us and why He lets things happen... Trust in GOD always though; because He knows why He is putting us through these things. One of His Promises is that He will NEVER leave us. Wait for the moment when you FEEL THE LORD has shown up. Because when Jesus shows up, everything changes. Infinite Joy is when His Peace comes. Jesus comes to save us, to GIVE us Salvation. It is but for The GRACE of GOD, that we are Chosen for this. This is why we must at all times remember to speak Life over Death.

Proverbs 18:21 reads: (KJV)

Death and Life are in the power of the tongue. : and they that love it shall eat the fruit thereof. Choose Life and Love. Speak GODLY things into our Lives. THE LORD spoke Earth and it was made, so were the stars and moon.

Don't let the Hope be gone, for you ARE a Child of GOD. GOD Loves you still, even in your worst days. He is still there with you, just open your eyes, ears and heart to "SEE" THE LORD. There is NO hopelessness in Heaven! Heaven is only Peace, Joy, Serenity, Mercy and Love.

Speaking Life GROWS things. A positive attitude with a kind word will end a conflict quicker.

Our Identity is "Who we are in Christ's Eyes." Let people see GOD'S Love in our daily words and actions. We also must call out "The Good of GOD" in others.

Pray this Prayer:

LORD, let me see things Your Way, with the Overflow of The Holy Spirit, (Hakuna matata-{NO WORRIES}). Always for Your Protection and Guidance, letting my heart, mind, body and soul be Yours to Lead.

In Jesus' Holy, Heavenly Name, we Pray!!! A-MEN!!!

PERFECT LOVE

He first Loved us!
1 John 4:15-19 (NIV)
3-8-2014

Never fear anything here on Earth, for GOD will protect you. If, however, it's Time for you to go home, how Glorious to say, "You can't hurt me, for I <u>AM</u> ready to go Home to my Heavenly Father!" Operate with fearless Love; for The Father Protects us at all times. We have the capacity to Preach anywhere and everywhere! Step ye out of your comfort zone and PREACH!!! WALK IN THE LORD'S FAVOR!!!

Love Me (GOD) in your Present Time, for this moment is all you have. The past doesn't make a difference, because I have washed all things anew! I will give you Inner Healing. Your Love and Faith have to work together! GOD

Proverbs 8:32-36 (KJV)

Now therefore hearken unto Me, O ye children: for Blessed are they that keep My Ways. Hear instruction, and be Wise, and refuse it not. Blessed is the man that heareth me, watching daily at My Gates, waiting at the posts of My doors. For whoso findeth Me findeth Life, and shall obtain Favor of

THE LORD. But he that sinneth against Me wrongeth his own soul: all they that hate Me love death.

Ephesians 5:1-2 and 8 (KJV)

Be ye therefore followers of GOD, as dear children; And walk in Love, as Christ also hath Loved us, and hath given Himself for us as an offering and a sacrifice to GOD for a sweet smelling Savour. For ye were sometimes darkness, but now are ye Light in THE LORD: walk as children of Light. Lev. 19:4, and 18 (KJV) Turn ye not unto idols, nor make to yourselves molten gods: I AM THE LORD, your God. Love thy neighbor as thyself.

Jesus' Love surpasses ALL understanding!!! Jesus never leaves us!!!

MY FINAL ACT

3-11-14

We often wonder where we will be when THE LORD calls us home. But we hardly realize the real mystery is accomplishing <u>what</u> THE LORD wants us to do with the short time He has given us here. We all need to remember to put Jesus first, letting the rest be in His Hands, to lead us where we are supposed to go and what He wants us to do in this life. Accomplishing this means that we need a closer walk with Jesus, Who is waiting to hear from us.

Psalms 16:7-11 NIV

Matt. 7:14 NIV

Because strait is The Gate, and narrow is the Way, which leadeth unto Life, and few there be that find it.

Psalm 16:1 NIV & Prayer

Preserve me, O GOD: for in thee do I put my trust.

Please, LORD, let my final act here be to call Your Name before You take me home.

THIS IS THE OPEN SEASON OF TRUE REPENTANCE!!!

3-4-2014

All of you are our future generation. The generation who is to bring home The Overflow of The New Blessings yet unseen. All we need is to believe that Jesus died for our sins and was raised from the grave and is Home with our Heavenly Father. Jesus has The Power to Change Lives. He alone can change Lives. For GOD alone is The Only One Who can Bless a mess.

True Repentance begins with accepting THE LORD as our Savior. This is John 3:16. Then begins the daily Walks with our LORD to learn more about Him and His Ways. These daily Walks are Bible Study, Meditation and fellowship with other Christians. Take your time to find a Church that is right for you. See if they have any Bible Studies during the week. If not, ask if they know of any Churches that do.

Remember, True Repentance is all about turning away from our old, sinful ways and making the choice to do what is right by following our LORD'S example. If ever in doubt, ask yourself, "What would Jesus do?" (W.W.J.D.?) If you are having trouble trying not to argue with someone, try "What would Jesus say?" (W.W.J.S.?)

Prayer is communicating with our LORD. Make Time during the day to have Quiet Time with THE LORD, preferably the same time each day, so that you won't forget.

Luke 9:23 NIV!!!

Blessed be your days!!! A-MEN!!!

FEAR

I am fearful of opening elevator doors. The reason is, I feel inadequate to take care of the person who is on the floor with medical issues (in labor or hurt) when the door opens. Will I have enough strength to help rather than to hurt? Will I have enough strength to be calm and peaceful? I fear opening the door to the public restrooms for the same reason. The person may be having a seizure, etc.. My biggest fear here is not being able to tell the 911 operator exactly what they need to know so that this person may be saved. I stutter and may not be able to say just the right information. I am fearful to make a mistake while Ministering, but THE LORD KNOWS these things and more about each of us. He is our Creator!!! Psalms 23:4 NIV

Even though I walk through the darkest valley, I will fear no evil, for You are with me; Your rod and Your staff, comfort me.

For THE LORD is with us wherever we go. Where we go, THE LORD also goes. Fear not, for I am with you.

When you are fearful, stop and Pray to Jesus for Him to "Just take this!". Give your problems to THE LORD and let Him take care of your problems for you. He is The Only One Who can fix your problems. We just have to have FAITH in Jesus that He will take care of it. In moments of need, Pray The Lord's Prayer Matthew 6:9-15 NIV.

Have a Blessed day!!!

SAVED AND UNSAVED

All NIV

There is no racism here. You are one or the other. You are either Saved and going to Heaven, or you are an unbeliever and going to Hell. There are NO gray areas.

STOP, DROP, AND ROLL DOESN'T WORK IN HELL!!!

Read all Scripture in your Bible:

1 Peter 1:2

Who have been chosen according to the foreknowledge of GOD The Father, through the sanctifying work of The Spirit, to be obedient to Christ Jesus and sprinkled with His blood: Grace and Peace be yours in abundance."... As a result, you have obeyed Him and have been cleansed by the blood of Jesus Christ.

1 Peter 1:8-10

Though you have not seen Him, you love Him; and even though you do not see Him now, you believe in Him and are filled with an inexpressible and glorious joy, for you are receiving the end result of your faith, the Salvation of your souls.

1 Peter 1:13-16

Therefore, with minds that are alert and fully sober, set your hope on the Grace to be brought to you when Jesus Christ is revealed at His coming. As obedient children, do not conform to the evil desires you had when you lived in ignorance. But just as He who called you is Holy, so be Holy in all you do; for it is written: "Be Holy, because I am Holy."

Leviticus 11:44

I am THE LORD your GOD; consecrate yourselves and be Holy, because I am Holy. Do not make yourselves unclean be any creature that moves along the ground. *** Repent your sins and be Saved!

2 Corinthians 6:17-18

Therefore, "Come out from them and be separate, says THE LORD. Touch no unclean thing, and I will receive you." And, "I will be a Father to you, and you will be My sons and daughters, says THE LORD ALMIGHTY."

Go from here, with the newness you now know, and Be Children of GOD!!!

In Jesus' Holy Name, we Pray!!! A-MEN!!!

PSALMS SUNDAY

Psalms 46:1 & 10 NIV
GOD is our Refuge and Strength, an
ever-present help in trouble.

Be still and KNOW that I AM GOD!!!

Wherever we are, we need also remember there also is THE LORD. A Perfect Time to tell someone of Jesus, is sharing with them what He's done for you. GOD is coming to visit us. Let us be ready when THE LORD comes to see us. Have we been Saved? Have others been Saved by our telling them about Jesus? Let us remember in any moment to give Praise to GOD. Pray for the good things He does for us and Pray also for the things to change from bad to great. Our days are numbered, so we must tell as many people as possible about The Coming of THE LORD. Please Pray for the unsaved, but also remember GOD wants us to Pray for our enemies. The day is coming soon when we will be at The Gates, then what do we say? I've done my share? Did Jesus give up on us before we were Saved? No, and HE won't give up on the unsaved either. Tell them to Pray this Prayer with you:

Dear LORD Jesus, i admit that i am a sinner. i believe Jesus died on The Cross for my sins. I'm truly sorry for my sins. Thank You for dying for me. Help me to Live as You would.

And Dear Jesus, Thank You for Hearing my Prayer this day and for Saving me. Now, please, help me to never be ashamed of You in front of others.

IN JESUS' HOLY, HEAVENLY
NAME WE PRAY!!! A-MEN!!!

EASTER SUNDAY

April 20, 2014

Jesus gave His all when He died on The Cross. You have to be Holy to be with GOD, so He sent His Only Son to wipe our sins clean. Isaiah 53:5 NIV

But He was pierced for our transgressions, He was crushed for our iniquities; the punishment that brought us Peace was upon Him, and by His wounds we are Healed.

Hebrews 10:18

And where these have been forgiven, sacrifice for sin is no longer necessary.

GOD'S Living Presence is now coming out. It is also called Grace, The Overflow of GOD'S Love.

Eph. 4:1-7, Mark 9:49, Is.60:19, 1 Thes. 5:5 (NIV) Walk in Salt and Light.

Eph. 3:17-19 NIV

Let Love and Mercy show in your Lives forever. Pray for The Power to understand and experience GOD'S Great Love!!!

Read Psalms 91 NIV

I love you. No, GOD'S deeply IN LOVE with us. He KNOWS how many hairs we have on our heads! He knows our souls and Spirits! BY THE GRACE OF GOD, HE <u>CHOSE</u> US TO BE HIS CHILDREN!!! He Loves us unconditionally (no matter what we've done).

Hebrews 10:11 NIV

When I stop <u>doing</u> it all by myself and let GOD do it, Grace Overflows. He calls us to Glorify Him by being His Children. Put your Faith in our LORD.

Let every day be a HOLY-day (Holiday)!!!

Pray this Prayer with me: LORD, I thank You so very much for being my Heavenly Father. Thank You for dying on The Cross for my sins. Help me to understand and experience Your Love. Thank You for Your Shield of Protection around me.

IN JESUS' HOLY, Heavenly NAME,
WE PRAY!!! A-MEN!!!

PRAYER

LORD, PLEASE BLESS ME WITH YOUR SPIRITUAL HELP!!!

Read NIV Psalms 28:1-9; 34:17; Psalms 141:1-2

I call to You, LORD, come quickly to me; hear me when I call to You. May my Prayer be set before You like incense; may the lifting up of my hands be like the evening sacrifice.

Dear LORD, please hear my cry! There are so many things going wrong in my Life today, and I don't know which way to turn. I feel so helpless. There is nothing I can do. Remember me, LORD, today as we meet in these moments of Prayer, for my problems are bigger than myself. Yes, truly I need Your Spiritual Help and Guidance at this moment in Time! I can't do this on my own.

(Tell THE LORD of your problems.)
I thank You for holding me close and never letting me go.

Joshua 1:5-9 NIV

THE LORD will never leave you nor forsake you. Be strong and very courageous.

Ps. 119:105 NIV

Your Word is a Lamp for my feet, a Light on my Path.

Psalm 68:4

Sing to God, sing in Praise of His Name, extol Him Who rides on the clouds; rejoice before Him - His Name is THE LORD.

Let THE LORD hold, keep, and guide you in all you do. May you find Peace, Joy, Grace and Mercy in our Heavenly Father's eyes.

In Jesus' Holy Name, we Pray!!! A-MEN!!!

AS I WALK

As my feet walk, I KNOW THE LORD leads me where He wants me to go. My Path for today will cross yours only if THE LORD is willing. But know this: when our paths cross, THE LORD will speak through me to tell you what He wants you to know. A Good Time to Minister is at hand. Ever stop at the gas station and tell someone about Jesus? Walmart? Every day is a new day that THE LORD has given us to Minister to the poor in Spirit, for we are only here for a short Time. We are not promised tomorrow. We need to do all we can to bring in The flock of lost ones (the ones who don't know Christ as their Savior, yet).

Romans 14:8 NIV

If we live, we live for THE LORD; and if we die, we die for THE LORD. So, whether we live or die, we belong to THE LORD.

Romans 8:1-2 & 14 NIV

Therefore, there is now no condemnation for those who are in Christ Jesus, because through Christ Jesus the law of The Spirit who gives life has set you free from the law of sin and death. For those who are led by The Spirit of GOD are the children of GOD.

Isaiah 61:1-3 NIV

The Spirit of The Sovereign Lord is upon me, because THE LORD has anointed me to proclaim good news to the poor. He has sent me to bind up the brokenhearted, to proclaim freedom for the captives and release from darkness for the prisoners, to proclaim the year of THE LORD's favor and the day of vengeance of our GOD, to comfort all who mourn, and provide for those who grieve in Zion- to bestow on them a crown of beauty instead of ashes, the oil of joy instead of mourning, and a garment of praise instead of a spirit of despair. They will be called oaks of righteousness, a planting of THE LORD, for the display of His splendor.

GO YE AND SPREAD THE WORD OF GOD!!! Guide my feet, Oh LORD, for I know not which way to go. Guide my mouth to say only as You would have me to say. Take me where You want me to go and Teach me to do what You want me to do. Heal my hurts as we go, so I will learn from where we have been. Let me learn how to Heal others as You would have me to do. Lead me where I go, for I will follow. I Love You, Jesus!!! Do with me as You will.

INSTRUCTIONS FOR CHRISTIAN HOUSEHOLDS

Ephesians 5:8-33 NIV

For you were once darkness, but now you are light in THE LORD. Live as children of light!!! (for the fruit of the light consists in all goodness, righteousness and truth) and find out what pleases THE LORD. Have nothing to do with the fruitless deeds of darkness, but rather expose them. It is shameful even to mention what the disobedient do in secret. But everything exposed by the light becomes visible-and everything that is illuminated becomes a light. This is why it is said: "Wake up, sleeper, rise from the dead and Christ will shine on you." Be very careful, then, how you Live, not as unwise but as wise, making the most of every opportunity, because the days are evil. Therefore do not be foolish, but understand what The LORD'S Will is. Do not get drunk on wine, which leads to debauchery (drunkenness); Instead be filled with The Holy Spirit, speaking to one another with Psalms, hymns, and songs from The Spirit. Sing and make music from your heart to THE LORD, always giving thanks to GOD, The Father, for everything, in The Name of our LORD Jesus Christ. Submit to one another out of reverence for Christ. Wives, submit yourselves to your own husbands as you do to THE LORD. For the husband is the head of the wife as Christ is the head of The Church; His Body, of which He is THE SAVOUR. Now as The Church submits to Christ, so also wives should submit to their husbands in everything. Husbands, love your wives, just as Christ loved The Church and gave Himself up for Her to make her Holy, cleansing her by the washing with water through The Word, and to present her to Himself as a radiant Church, without stain or wrinkle or any other blemish, but Holy and Blameless: In this same way, husbands ought to Love their wives as their own bodies. He who loves his wife, loves himself. After all, no one ever hated their own body, but they feed and care for their body, just as Christ does The Church for we are members of His Body. "For this reason, a man will leave his father and mother and be united to his wife, and the two will become one flesh." This is a profound mystery-but I am talking about Christ and The Church. However, each one of you also must love his wife as he loves himself, and the wife must respect her husband.

LORD, let me be more and more humble, that I might see. Help me to understand what You want me to do. Let me walk in Thine Path always, Father.

IN JESUS' HOLY NAME, we PRAY!!! A-MEN!!!

THE LORD BE WITH YOU!!!

Forgive Kate-Integrity!!!
I do forgive you Little Katie! It wasn't your fault. I miss you!
Psalms 46:1 NIV
GOD is our Refuge and Strength, a
very present help in trouble.
LET CHRIST OVERFLOW THROUGH YOU!!!

1 Thes. 5:16-18 NIV

Rejoice always, Pray continually, give thanks in all circumstances; for this is GOD'S Will for you in Christ Jesus.

Isaiah 61:1-3; and Isaiah 11:2 NIV

Inner Healing begins with letting Jesus in (accepting THE LORD as your Savior), for He first Loved us before we were even thought of by anyone here on Earth. Live and let GOD!!! Let GOD do all your Healing, for He alone best knows how to Heal us. He knows the exact kind of Healing each of us needs. He is patching us up so that we may overflow with His Righteousness and be more Christ-like. In all we do, we are here only to Glorify GOD for The Blessings in our Lives and the Lives of those we Love. Participate with Christ in helping someone to be set free, as we are. Using Compassion for others, we can show them the Loving kindness of how it is to be Saved.

GO FROM HERE SPREAD THE
WORD: JESUS SAVES!!!
IN JESUS' HOLY NAME, we PRAY!!! A-MEN!!!

THANK YOU, LORD!!!

March 2, 2015

Thank You, LORD, for waking me up this morning!!! Today is a day You Truly have made just for me. It is so beautiful here with the sun shining and the weather is not so bad outside.

My Brothers and Sisters in Christ were already at Worship when I got there, but I wasn't late. I am part of the team that has things to do before others come, like getting coffee ready, tidying up and such. I Love when THE LORD awakens me early so I can go help.

We are Children of God gathered together for Worship!!! Oh, what could be better today? I Love going through my day in anticipation of what THE LORD has in store for me. Where will He lead my feet today? Who does He want me to talk to and what does He want me to say? Where does He want me to go? I'm ready to go. Wherever You want me, is wherever I will be. I always want to encourage and empower you to share GOD'S Holy Word.

May Peace, Joy, Grace and Mercy be yours forever.
In Jesus' Holy Name, we Pray!!! A-MEN!!!

THE AWESOME POWER OF GOD!!!

Jesus is The Ultimate Unifier!!!

The seniors are the future generation of Jesus. The seniors are the ones who have learned by their parent's generation who Jesus IS. The ones who have been in Church the longest know The Word of GOD. These are our next Generation for Christ. They already have been Teaching, but who was listening? Our generation should have listened to the oldest generation. THE LORD'S wise men and women are sent to instruct us on Christian Living, therefore we need to listen, as The Kingdom of THE LORD, our GOD, is at hand.

Remember Matthew 5:1-16 NIV

Blessed are they that Hear The Word of GOD and obey.

1 Peter 2:9-10 (KJV)

But you are a Chosen People, a Royal Priesthood, an Holy Nation, a peculiar people; that ye should shew forth The Praises of Him Who hath Called you out of the darkness into

His marvelous Light. Which in Time past were not a people, but are now the people of GOD: which had not obtained Mercy, but now having obtained Mercy.

WE ARE THE CHOSEN GENERATION!!! As well we learn, we need to Teach our children and grandchildren, lest they fall by the wayside and never see the pearly Gates of Heaven!!!

GO YE FROM HERE AND SPREAD THE WORD YOU HAVE HEARD!!! KNOW WHO YOU ARE IN CHRIST!!! In Jesus' Name, Bless you; for you are The Teachers of GOD'S Children.

NEVER FORGET WHO YOU ARE
IN CHRIST'S EYES!!!

LIVE IN THE OVERFLOW

May 25, 2014

Ask GOD in your Prayers to guide your feet and mouth to do what He wants you to do today. The Holy Spirit released His courage upon us this day. All each of us has to do is accept The Blessing as it is. One of the many Blessings yet to come. Let us each have confidence when we approach our Heavenly Father's Throne. Another Blessing for us. Just to approach The Father's Throne is a Blessing, but to know that we are Loved and accepted, as who we are, when we get there is a True Blessing. Ask GOD to overflow your Life. Ask Him to show you your Divine Destiny for today. I am a testimony of GOD to others. He wants to overflow my Life, so I can overflow other's Lives also. As we are led through this day with the protection of THE LORD!!! Let us ask this: How may I today, LORD, be of the most service to You and Your Kingdom? Please let my feet and my mouth follow Your direction for me.

IN JESUS' HOLY NAME, we PRAY!!! A-MEN!!!

WALKING IN FAITH

July 2, 2014

Faith without deeds is useless. We walk in Faith, not by sight.
Micah 7:7-10 (KJV)

But as for me, I watch in Hope for THE LORD, I wait for
GOD, my SAVIOR, my GOD will hear me. Do not gloat over
me, O mine enemy! Though I have fallen, I will rise. Though I
sit in darkness, THE LORD will be my Light. Because I have
sinned against Him, I will bear THE LORD'S Wrath, until
He pleaded my case and upholds my cause. He will bring me
out into The Light; I will see His Righteousness. Then my
enemy will see it and will be covered in shame, she who said
to me, 'Where is THE LORD, your God?" My eyes will see
her downfall; even now she will be trampled underfoot like
mire in the streets.

Ps.107:1-7 NIV

Give Thanks to THE LORD, for He is Good; His Love
endures forever. Let The Redeemed of THE LORD tell their
story: those He redeemed from the hand of the foe, those
He gathered from the lands, from east and west, from north
and south, some wandered in the desert wastelands, finding

no way to a city where they could settle. They were hungry and thirsty, and their lives ebbed away. Then they cried out to THE LORD in their trouble, and He delivered them from their distress. He led them by a straight way to a city where they could settle.

Matthew 5:5 NIV

Blessed are the meek, for they will inherit the earth.

A-MEN!!!

A BIBLE STORY

July 2, 2014

Psalms 7:15-16 KJV

Whoever digs a hole and scoops it out; falls into the pit they have made. 16 The trouble they cause recoils on them; their violence comes down on their own heads.

Jeremiah 1:5-9 NIV

Before I formed you in The Womb, I knew you, before you were born, I set you apart; I appointed you as a prophet to the nations." 6 "Alas, Sovereign LORD," I said, "I do not know how to speak; I am too young." 7 But THE LORD said to me, "Do not say, 'I am too young.' You must go to everyone I send you to and say whatever I command you. 8 Do not be afraid of them, for I am with you and will rescue you," declares THE LORD. 9 Then THE LORD reached out HIS Hand and touched my mouth and said to me, "I have put My Words in your mouth."

Read both Psalms 3 and 4 NIV. Sleep well, for you are very well protected by THE LORD.

Psalms 34:4

I sought THE LORD, and He answered me; He delivered me from ALL my fears.

Psalms 119:105-106 NIV

Your Word is a lamp for my feet, a light on my Path; 106: I have taken an oath and confirmed it that I will follow Your Righteous Laws.

Matthew 5:9 NIV

Blessed are the peacemakers, for they will be called Children of GOD.

THE LORD'S Prayer - Matthew 6:9-15 NIV
Luke 11:2-10; and 33-36 NIV
Matt. 7:7-8 NIV Ask, Seek and Knock
John 21:25 NIV AND OUR OWN TESTIMONY?

Remember always: Jesus Loves us all. Feed HIS sheep well until HIS return. Study the Bible carefully. Psalms 51:7 NIV

Revelation 22:21 NIV
THE GRACE OF OUR LORD JESUS
CHRIST BE WITH YOU ALL.

A-MEN!!!

OUR WEIGHT
IN GOLD

September 2, 2014

Seriously, we all say, "I wish I had my weight paid to me in gold." But, really, why? All the gold you can carry could be yours, but if you are not Saved, what would it matter? You could have the gold and die the very next second. Would that have accomplished anything? No.

When we set up our treasures in Heaven, we need to remember that these things are Eternal and Everlasting. For our treasures here on earth are about helping our sister or brother where and when they need help, not expecting any returns.

Our Integrity is our Gold. How does GOD see us? What would He say about what we are doing? Would He say we have learned well or would we need to study more? We all need to study more to be closer with our LORD. Our example to follow is Jesus. If He wouldn't do something, then why should we? What happened to helping our neighbors through the rough times? To give a little from your Heart, not because you had to, but because you saw a need.

We are called here to SERVE. This week I wore an apron to Church, because THE LORD said so. He uses things like this to open doors to Preach to the listening ones (the ones who ask). "Why are you wearing the apron," I am asked. I tell them that we are here to Serve one another.

So, this week, please let THE LORD show you how to Serve someone. It's simple, you see a need and you help. Just opening a door for someone. Smile at them, as you do. These are our rewards.

I Pray, Lord, that You open their eyes to see the good that they can do for each other and the rewards that can be theirs. Open their mouths to speak only Yours Words, of Peace and Joy. Let them be filled this week, with Your Holy Spirit.

In Jesus Name, I Pray. A-MEN!!!
May you go from here and Spread The Holy Word!!!

INFINITE LOVE

May 25, 2014
Ephesians 2:4-10 and 13(KJV)

But GOD, Who is rich in mercy, for HIS Great Love wherewith He Loved us, [5]Even when we were dead in sins, hath quickened us together with Christ, (by Grace ye are Saved); [6]And hath raised us up together, and made us sit together in Heavenly Places in Christ Jesus: [7]That in the ages to come He might shew the exceeding riches of His Grace in His Kindness toward us through Christ Jesus. [8]For by Grace are ye Saved through Faith; and that not of yourselves: it is The Gift of God. [9]Not of work, lest any man should boast. [10]For we are His Workmanship, created in Christ Jesus unto Good Works, which GOD hath before ordained that we should walk in them (The Good Works). ([13])But now in Christ Jesus, ye who sometimes were far off, are made nigh by The Blood of Christ.

Ephesians 3:17-18

That Christ may dwell in your hearts by Faith; that ye, being rooted and grounded in Love, [18]May be able to comprehend with all Saints what is the breadth, and length, and depth, and height; [19]And to Know the Love of Christ, Which surpasseth knowledge, that ye might be filled with all The Fullness of GOD.

Psalm 103:8 KJV

THE LORD is merciful and Gracious: slow to anger, and plenteous in mercy.

Psalms 107:8-9 KJV

Oh that men would Praise THE LORD for His Goodness, and for His Wonderful Works to the children of men! [9]For He Satisfieth the longing of soul, and filleth the hungry soul with Goodness.

Psalms 117:1 KJV

O Praise THE LORD, all ye nations: Praise Him, all ye people. For His merciful kindness is great toward us: and the truth of THE LORD endureth for ever. Praise ye THE LORD.

Praise The Lord!!!

WORDS OF THE WISE

9/29/14

Proverbs 20:12 NIV

Ears that hear and eyes that see-THE LORD has made them both.

Proverbs 21:1-2 NIV

The Righteous One takes note of the house of the wicked and brings the wicked to ruin.

Proverbs 21:21-22 NIV

Whoever pursues Righteousness and Love finds Life, Prosperity, and Honor. One who is wise can go up against the city of the mighty and pull down the stronghold with which they trust.

Proverbs 22:11 NIV

One who Loves a pure heart and who speaks with Grace will have The King for a friend.

Proverbs 23:4 & 5 NIV

Do not wear yourself out to get rich; do not trust your own cleverness. Cast but a glance at riches, and they are gone, for they will surely sprout wings and fly off to the sky like an eagle.

Proverbs 23:12 NIV

Apply your heart to instruction and your ears to Words of Knowledge.

Proverbs 20:3 NIV

It is to one's honor to avoid strife, but every fool is quick to quarrel.

A person who is truly confident of his or her strength does not need to parade it. A truly brave person does not look for chances to prove it. A resourceful woman can find a way out of a fight!!! A man of endurance will avoid retaliating. Foolish people find it impossible to avoid strife.

MEN AND WOMEN OF CHARACTER CAN AND WILL!!! What kind of person are you??? Blessed be the ones who hear these words and listen!!!

GRACE, MERCY, PEACE, LOVE TO ALL!!!
IN JESUS' HOLY NAME!!! A-MEN!!

FLOCK OF THE LOST SHEEP

John 10:7-18 (NIV)

Therefore Jesus said again, "Very truly I tell you, I am the gate for the sheep. All who have come before Me are thieves and robbers, but the sheep have not listened to them. I am the gate; whoever enters through Me will be Saved. They will come in and go out, and find pasture. The thief comes only to steal and kill and destroy; I have come that they may have life, and have it to the full. I am The good Shepherd. The good Shepherd lays down His life for the sheep. The hired hand is not the shepherd and does not own the sheep. So when he sees the wolf coming, he abandons the sheep and runs away. Then the wolf attacks the flock and scatters it. The man runs away because he is a hired hand and cares nothing for the sheep. I am the good Shepherd; I know My Sheep and My sheep know Me-just as the Father knows Me and I know the Father- and I lay down My Life for the sheep. I have other sheep that are not of this sheep pen. I must bring them also. They too will listen to My voice, and there shall be one flock and one Shepherd. The reason My Father Loves Me is that I lay down My Life-only to take it up again. No one takes it from Me, but I lay it down of My own accord. I have authority to lay it down and authority to take it up again. This command I received from My Father.

John 10:25-30 NIV

Jesus answered "I did tell you, but you do not believe. The works I do in My Father's name testify about Me, but you do not believe because you are not My sheep. My sheep listen to My Voice; I know them, and they follow Me. I give them Eternal Life, and they shall never perish; no one will snatch them out of My hand. My Father, who has given them to Me, is greater than all; no one can snatch them out of my Father's Hand. I and the Father are one.

PRAY THIS PRAYER:

Come one and all to The Grace of GOD, because we all have sinned. We humbly ask your forgiveness for our wrongs. We ask that from this day forward that you guide our steps, so we may do as You would want us to do for You. Thank You for dying on The Cross for us. Thank You for The Blessings only You can Give.

IN JESUS' HOLY NAME, I PRAY!!! A-MEN!!!

TRAINING OUR DAUGHTERS

February 4, 2015

First, I must say, we, (Ladies of GOD), have to learn the meaning of "I am Yours. I am forever Yours." We are the chosen ones to teach our daughters who they are in Christ. They also are the chosen ones for The Kingdom of GOD.

Titus 2:1-5 NIV Show by Example!

¹You, however, must teach what is appropriate to sound doctrine.

²Teach the older men to be temperate, worthy of respect, self controlled, and sound in Faith, in Love and in endurance.

³Likewise, teach the older women to be reverent in the way they live, not to be slanderers or addicted to much wine, but to teach what is good.

⁴Then they can urge the younger women to Love their husbands and children,

⁵to be self-controlled and pure, to be busy at home, to be kind, and to be subject to their husbands, so that no one will malign The Word of GOD.

Train your child up not to fear anything. Teach them Integrity - "A How To" for THE LORD. Teach them how to dress for THE LORD, how to Speak The Word of GOD, and only the things of THE LORD must we teach them.

THE LORD'S Grace has given us enough Time to teach them, but hurry, for we all are not promised tomorrow. We may not be here tomorrow to teach them The Integrity or Grace of GOD! We must teach each other also The Integrity of THE LORD. If Jesus would NOT do something, then WHY should we? Who did Jesus learn from? He looked up and saw The Father do this, therefore I will do it. Think about the things we have heard Jesus DO because He saw Our Father DO them. Healings - Rise and go, for your Faith has Healed you.

Read 2 Timothy 1:7-10; Jeremiah 29:11-14; and Psalm 40:5

A-MEN!!!

STOMPING OUT SATAN!!!

March 4, 2015
(All NIV)

GOD BLESS OUR FIREFIGHTERS!!! DIXIE WILL NEVER BURN again!!! Dixie is considered everywhere South of the Mason/Dixon Line. The fire (racism) that was started years ago, is the one we (The Firefighters - Christians) are sent here to stomp out. We no longer agree with what our grandfathers' forefathers' did. I mean (really) that's how long it's been.

Read: Exodus 20:5 (NIV)

We are THE LORD'S Children!!! Seen by GOD as His!!! THE LORD is jealous for us. Learning, as we Live in this world, that we are not from this world. One day, we will all go Home and have to account for our own words and actions while we were here.

We here in the South have come to stomp out racism.

We start this journey by reading Proverbs 2:1-9; Matthew 5:3-12; and forgetting not Luke 6:35-38.

When we read these, re-read them many times to really understand them, then practice them in all we do.

Whoever is reading this today, LORD, please Bless them and their families, in Your good health, understanding and wisdom.

In Jesus Name, we Pray!!! A-MEN!!!

IS THE WILDERNESS JOURNEY OVER?

March 13, 2015
OUR JOURNEY BEGINS HERE:

Read John 13:14-17 (NIV)

Now that you know these things, you will be Blessed if you do them.

John 4:34 NIV

"My Food," says Jesus, "is to do The Will of Him Who sent Me and to finish His Work."

John 6:38-40 NIV

For I have come down from Heaven not to do My Will but to do The Will of Him Who sent Me. And this is The Will of Him Who sent Me, that I shall lose none of all those He has given Me, but raise them up at The Last Day. For My Father's Will is that everyone who looks to The Son and Believes in Him shall have Eternal Life, and I will raise them up The Last Day.

John 6:44-45 NIV

"No one can come to Me unless The Father Who sent Me draws them, and I will raise them up at The Last Day. It is written in The Prophets: 'They will all be taught by God. Everyone who has heard The Father and learned from Him comes to Me.

John 7:16 NIV

My Teaching is not My Own. It comes from The One Who sent Me.

Just think!!! He Who sent me!!! How Amazing!!! But it is said that as I have been sent, now, I send you. We are The New Disciples of Christ now. We must show everyone by our own example of Who Jesus is.

John 16 teaches us not to worry about being guided through this world. We have The Holy spirit as our Guide.

The Blessings are yet to come.

We need just remember to: Have no other gods before Me and do unto others as we would have them to do unto us.

Spreading Joy, Peace, Kindness and Love to all.
IN JESUS' HOLY, HEAVENLY
NAME, we PRAY!!! A-MEN!!!

HOW TO FISH?!

March 19, 2015

THE LORD is Teaching me today to learn to listen to Him and enjoy Him wherever He is. My husband and I were going fishing today, but we had to stop at The Curb Market for a fishing license for me and some more things. (Worms to catch the bait.) Then on to a friend's to fish for the bait. A great Time to Minister (by the way). We leave here and go to a store in Burnsville (the middle of nowhere).

My husband was heating the food we were buying, the customer left, the cashier went to help my husband, and I had just come from the bathroom. Nothing really, everything was normal. Then THE LORD came and danced with me and my arms just DANCED AND SO DID MY FEET!!! Nothing abnormal to me, but I heard the cashier giggle and ask, "What was that?" Yeah, that wasn't normal, but what a Time to Minister. Just by Dancing with THE LORD!!!

We then leave there and go to The Lock and Dam. On the way, my husband is whining because he doesn't have the bait. Live fish. I tell him to be quiet and wait. I tell him it is like GOD is saying, "The bait is already there." So, when we get there, I get ALL the stuff to tote down the hill ready. I take down the first load, and there are the live bait, swimming in a little water hole. I go back up and help bring down the rest of the stuff. My husband rigs up both his poles and starts fishing. Then he rigs up both my fishing poles and I start fishing. He goes up the hill to the bathroom. I catch a fish while he's gone, but I couldn't catch it. He comes back and I tell him to catch it, because I'm afraid to break the line. He gives it back shortly, afraid he's gonna break the line, and needing to fish with his own poles. I wrestle with it and THE LORD showed me that this is what He was showing me:

1. That the fishing poles worked fine. Nothing was wrong with them.
2. That I, Leese, was not a fisherman, but a Fisherwoman. That I am a Fisher of Men. Both are Peaceful. The Fisherman has Time with THE LORD. I have all the Time to do for THE LORD. THE LORD told me not to worry about whether or not I could actually catch the fish, because I am A Fisher of Men. GOD Himself will catch and clean the men.

Thank You, LORD, for today and all the other days.

IN JESUS NAME, we PRAY!!! A-MEN!!!

HOLD YOUR HEAD UP AND REST IN THE LORD!!!

SPEAK IT INTO EXISTENCE!!! We all have the Power to speak good things into our lives. We have the power to do evil also, so please remember to speak only good things over people. Your enemy is the one to be prayed over more, because it seems the more good we do (Jesus through us), the more the attack IS ON!!! We all truly go through things that we feel are like the end of this world, and that Jesus is not there; but by THE GRACE OF GOD, HE has never left us AND NEVER WILL!!! He, by His Grace, chose to stay with us!!! We may be in that "pit", but remember -- Joy comes in the morning!!!

Who is going to Heaven? ONLY THE SAVED!!! Your Grace is enough for me. This is the Open Season of True Repentance. For you are ALL the Next Generation. All you need is Jesus!!! He has The Power to change lives!!! This is where Mom and Dad should be raising their children as Children of GOD!!! Please put the earthly things behind your families before it's too late to save your Souls over the electronical generations' gadgets; E-boxes, cell phones, computers and such. Some of us are no longer a Generation of GOD'S Children. But this is what we need to do:

1. Keep our focus on our LORD!!! Matthew 6:33 (NIV)
2. Keep THE LORD'S Commandments Ex. 20:1-17 NIV
3. Practice your <u>Daily Walk with THE LORD!!!</u>
4. Do unto others as you would have them do to you. Use the Compassionate Love of Christ while thinking before doing. Luke 6:31 NIV

Pray that THE LORD reveals His Plan for our Lives. Let Him reveal how our walk is to be today. Who do we need to tell about You, today, LORD?

REMEMBER ALL WE DO HERE IS
TO GLORIFY THE LORD!!!

FASTING FROM
THE BIBLE

(All NIV)

Fasting in The Bible generally means going without all food and drink for a period of time and not merely refraining from certain foods. Fasting in The Old Testament was often directed towards securing The Guidance and Help of GOD. Some came to think that fasting would automatically gain man favor by hearing from GOD.

Read Isaiah 58:3-12 (NIV)

Against this The Prophets declared that without RIGHT conduct, fasting was in vain. In The New Testament

The only occasion when Jesus is recorded as fasting is at the Time of His Temptations in the wilderness. However, He was not necessarily fasting from choice. The first temptation implies that there was no food available in the place where He had selected for His weeks of preparation for His Ministry. "(Matthew 4:1-4; Moses fast - (Ex. 34:28) and Elijah (1 Kings 19:8).

Jesus assumed that His Hearers would fast; but He taught them when they did so to face God-ward, not man-ward.

Read: Matthew 6:16-18; Matthew 9-14-17; Mark 2:18-22; Luke 5:33-39) Later they would fast like others.

In Acts: Choosing Missionaries (13:2-3); and elders (14:23) and Paul refers to his fasting in

2 Corinthians 6:5; voluntary fasting, by way of self-discipline, (Matthew 17:21; Mark 9:29; Acts 10:30; 1 Corinthians 7:5) indicates a growing belief in the value of fasting in the early Church. How to Fast

Esther 9:31 (Instructions for Times of Fasting) Matthew 6:16-18 (Do not show man that you fast) Isaiah 58:54 (Kind of Fasting)

Also others: Matthew 9:14-15; Mark 2:18-20; Luke 5:33-35

Regularly: Luke 2:37; Luke 7:33; Luke 18:12; and Matthew 11:18; Zech. 7:3, 5

Fasting the Fifth and Seventh months:

Zech. 8:19

Fasts of the Fourth, Fifth; Seventh, and Tenth month will become Joy. It is (in my opinion) pointless to fast, unless you fast to be able to get closer to GOD and He, THE LORD, closer to you. This is part of your Walk with THE LORD that you must NOT share with ANYONE!!! This fast is to show your Love for THE LORD in a way to grow closer to THE LORD to understand Him better and to better KNOW what is your own Divine Destiny.

May you all find your Walk with THE LORD as Peaceful as it is meant to be.

In Jesus' Holy Name, I Pray!!! A-MEN!!!

TEN COMMANDMENTS

March 24, 2015

EXODUS 20:1-21(NIV)

And GOD spoke all these words:

"I am THE LORD your GOD, who brought you out of Egypt, out of the land of slavery." "You shall have no other gods before Me."

"You shall not make for yourself an image in the form of anything in Heaven above or on the Earth beneath or in the waters below.

You shall not bow down to them or worship them; for I, THE LORD your GOD, am a jealous GOD punishing the children for the sin of the parents to the third and fourth generation of those who hate Me, but showing Love to a thousand [generations] of those who Love Me and keep My Commandments."

"You shall not misuse The Name of THE LORD your GOD, for THE LORD will not hold anyone guiltless who misuses His Name."

"Remember The Sabbath day by keeping it Holy. Six days you shall labor and do all your work, but The seventh day is a Sabbath to THE LORD your GOD. On it you shall not do any work, neither you, nor your son or daughter, nor your male or female servant, nor your animals, nor any foreigner residing in your towns. For in six days THE LORD made The Heavens and the earth, the sea, and all that is in them, but He rested on the seventh day. Therefore THE LORD Blessed The Sabbath day and made it Holy."

"Honor your father and your mother, so that you may live long in the land THE LORD your GOD is giving you." "You shall not murder."

"You shall not commit adultery."

"You shall not steal."

"You shall not give false testimony against your neighbor."

"You shall not covet your neighbor's house. You shall not covet your neighbor's wife, or his male or female servant, his ox or donkey, or anything that belongs to your neighbor."

When the people saw the thunder and lightning and heard the trumpet and saw the mountain in smoke, they trembled with fear. They stayed at a distance and said to Moses, "Speak to us yourself and we will listen. But do not have GOD speak to us or we will die."

Moses said to the people, "Do not be afraid. GOD has come to test you, so that the fear of GOD will be with you to keep you from sinning."

The people remained at a distance, while Moses approached the thick darkness where GOD was. Galatians 2:15-16 (NIV) This is why we should still obey them.

So we, too, have put our Faith in Christ Jesus that we may be justified by Faith in Christ and not by the works of the law, because by the works of the law no one will be justified.

COLOSSIANS 3:16 "LET CHRIST'S
WORD DWELL IN YOU RICHLY!!!"

RESURRECTION SUNDAY (EASTER)

April 8, 2015

Luke 24:5 NIV

Why do you look for the living among the dead? Why are <u>we</u> still looking for Someone WHO IS ALIVE (JESUS) among the dead? Jesus is alive wherever you go, all you have to is believe and ask THE LORD for your eyes and heart to be opened. Not only the eyes on your face, but the eyes of your soul.

JESUS IS RISEN!!!
The Greatest Story ever told; The Tomb is empty.

Matthew 2:1 (NIV) Jesus was born in Bethlehem.

John 3:16 (NIV) For GOD so Loved the world that He GAVE His one and only Son, that whoever Believes in Him shall not perish but have Eternal Life.

John 10:10 (NIV) The thief comes only to steal and kill and destroy; I have come that they may have Life, and have it abundantly.

Good Friday is fulfillment of The Bible - John 3:16 (NIV)

EASTER SUNDAY

HE IS ALIVE AND RISEN!!!

He remains ALIVE in us as we Share who we KNOW HE IS!!! He overcame death for our sins, so that we may receive Salvation, freely given to us by our LORD and Saviour, Jesus Christ.

Matthew 10:8 (All NIV)

Freely you have received; freely give. He alone <u>IS</u> The One Who paid The Price for our sin and our Salvation.

<u>Our KING is above all other kings.</u>

No one before You, LORD, was ever like You and none shall copy You. The Power to CHANGE Lives is all Yours!!! Thank You for Changing mine!!!

HE REDEEMED US!!!

The Cross was a symbol of Loving Payment for our sins, for us to be able to be Redeemed. Our Father has Promised to take care of us, (HIS Children). Jesus died for us so that we could become Heirs of Heaven with Jesus. This is The New Covenant: cut in Blood by Jesus. The Bread and The Wine are so we can be ONE with Jesus, Co-heirs in The Kingdom of GOD!!! We are made righteous by Jesus to be Sons and Daughters of The Most High!!! The old Covenant was about man's work-How well did we perform? The New Covenant-Jesus died for our sins.

Hebrews 13:20 (NIV)

Now may The GOD of Peace, Who through The Blood of The Eternal Covenant brought back from the dead our LORD Jesus, that Great Shepherd of The Sheep, equip you with everything good for doing His Will, and may He work in us what is pleasing to Him through Jesus Christ, to whom be Glory for ever and ever!!! A-MEN!!!

His Shalom Peace makes us complete. Jesus came to make us complete. He sees us as a forgiven Son or Daughter, because He gave us His Holy Spirit, who works in us to set us free. Jesus is "all-in" for us. The Holy Spirit does the work so we may be able to have a personal relationship with our LORD, Jesus Christ in our Daily Walk with Him.

READ PSALMS 19 NIV

H.M.M.-SOMETHING TO THINK ABOUT!!!

April 12, 2015

A little Love and Compassion can go a long way.

Consideration of someone else's feelings before your own feelings shows maturity and wisdom. Grace and Forgiveness was shown to us, therefore let us show our Grace and Forgiveness to others for The Glory of GOD'S Kingdom.

GOD wants each one of our hearts to shine brightly for Him!!!

BE THOU MY VISION, LORD OF ALL!!!
BELIEVING GOD IS GOOD, AND
HE CHANGES LIVES!!!

H.M.M.-Something to Think About!!!
April 16, 2015

We both live and understand from our own life's experiences. What you say, feel and do are important to me. What I say, feel and do should be important to you.

What we each say and do must be in heart-felt compassion
for the other: with the Love of Christ as the beginning..

We must each be aware of the other's feelings, thoughts, and
needs and point of view to communicate well with the other.

Let us each have open eyes and hearts full
of Love for one another by GOD'S Grace
and Mercy for HIS Kingdom's Glory.

H.M.M.-Something to Think About!!!
May 9, 2015

Don't cut corners building anything, for the
home you build may be your own.

A man worked his whole life for one family as a construction
worker. Upon wanting to retire, his employers asked him to
do one last thing for them. They wanted him to build them
a mansion. He cut corners by buying low-grade wood, and
cheap materials, because he wanted to retire from all work.
He finished the mansion, and they gave it to him as his own.

MORAL OF THE STORY IS:
If you are going to do anything; do it to your
best. Give your best effort in all you do.

GUIDES-(TEACHERS)

May 21, 2015

Psalms 119:105-106 (NIV)

Thy word is a Lamp unto my feet, and a Light unto my Path. I have taken an oath and confirmed it, that I will follow Your Righteous Laws.

LORD, Lead me where You want me to go and show me how to do what You want me to do Guides - Be Tour Guides as well as Teachers, for I, Your GOD, have made both for their own reason; each has their own purpose.

*** First, you must Listen or you will wander with no Destiny.

*** Second, Guides will lead you to your Teachers. I have picked your Destiny out for you, for it is the closest part of your Heart, nearest you. This is your dearest dream. Follow only GOD'S lead, for only GOD CAN Lead.

*** Third, live the life THE LORD gives us to the fullest, because He gave and chose us to live this life to spread His Word; any and ALL ways we can. Let us find new ways today to Spread Christ's Holy Word of Salvation!!!

John 16:7-13 NIV THE HOLY SPIRIT WILL COME!!!

The Counselor Teaches us, so we can Teach others, for Christ Himself says so in verses Matthew 28:18-20 NIV.

Then Jesus came to them and said, "All Authority in Heaven and on Earth has been given to Me. Therefore go and make disciples of all nations, baptising them in The Name of The Father and The Son and of The Holy Spirit, and teaching them to obey everything that I have commanded you. And surely I am with you always, to the very end of the age."

GO AND SPREAD THE HOLY WORD OF CHRIST!!!

IN JESUS' HOLY, HEAVENLY
NAME, we PRAY!!! A-MEN!!!

LOVE FULFILLS
THE LAW

April 27, 2015

Romans 13:8-14 NIV

Let no debt remain outstanding, except the continuing debt to
Love one another, for whoever Loves others has fulfilled the law.
The Commandments, "You shall not commit adultery," "You
shall not murder," "You shall not steal," "You shall not covet", and
whatever other Command there may be, are summed up in this
one Command: "Love your neighbor as yourself. Love does no
harm to a neighbor. Therefore Love is the fulfillment of the law.

And do this, understanding the present Time: The hour has
already come for you to wake up from your slumber, because
our Salvation is nearer now than when we first believed; The
night is nearly over; The day is almost here. So let us put aside
the deeds of darkness and put on the armor of Light. Let
us behave decently, as in the daytime; not in carousing and
drunkenness, not in sexual immorality and debauchery, not
in dissension and jealousy. Rather, clothe yourselves with The
LORD Jesus Christ, and do not think about how to gratify the
desires of the flesh. Paul considers attitudes just as important

as actions. Just as hatred leads to murder, so jealousy leads to strife and lust to adultery.

When Christ returns, He wants to find His People clean inside and out.

Heavenly Father, we Pray for Your Guidance for us. Guide our mouths and Hearts, LORD, as we Pray our feet to do well at the Task set before us. We thank You, LORD, for Choosing us to be in Heaven with You forever!!! Thank You for sending Your Son to die on The Cross for our sins.

WE LOVE YOU, LORD!!!
In Jesus Name we Pray!!! A-MEN!!!

BE CAREFUL OF WHAT YOU DO.

April 28, 2015

Proverbs 1:10-19 (NIV)

My son, if sinners entice you, do not give in to them. If they say, "Come along with us; let's lie in wait for someone's blood, let's waylay some harmless soul; let's swallow them alive, like the grave, and whole, like those who go down to the pit; we will get all sorts of valuable things and fill our houses with plunder; throw in your lot with us, we will all share the loot"-- my son, do not go along with them, do not set foot on their paths; for their feet rush into sin, they are swift to shed blood. How useless to spread a net where every bird can see it! These men lie in wait for their own blood; they ambush only themselves! Such are the paths of all who go after ill-gotten gain; it takes away the life of those who get it.

FOCUS ON GOD

JULY 6, 2015
Focus on God, our ALL in ALL!!!
Deuteronomy 32:1-4 NIV

Listen, you Heavens, and I will speak; hear, you earth, the words of my mouth. Let my Teaching fall like rain and my words descend like dew, like showers on new grass, like abundant rain on tender plants. I will proclaim The Name of The LORD. Oh, Praise the greatness of our GOD! He is The Rock, His Works are Perfect, and all His Ways are just. A Faithful GOD who does no wrong, upright and just is He. We serve GOD - not this world. Because Jesus Rules!!! Jesus died on The Cross for our sins, therefore we are made Righteous.

Romans 6:18-19 NIV

You have been set free from sin and have become slaves to righteousness. I am using an example from everyday life because of your human limitations. Just as you used to offer yourselves as slaves to impurity and to ever increasing wickedness, so now offer yourselves as slaves to Righteousness leading to Holiness. We are complete and whole when we Walk in Righteousness. Walk out your Completeness. Be the new person who understands that you have a Destiny!!!

2 Corinthians 5:17-20 NIV

Therefore, if anyone is in Christ, the new creation has come; the old has gone, the new is here! All this is from GOD, who reconciled us to Himself through Christ and gave us The Ministry of Reconciliation: that GOD was reconciling the world to Himself in Christ, not counting the people's sin against them. And He has committed to us this message of reconciliation. We are therefore Christ's Ambassadors, as though GOD were making His Appeal through us. We implore you on Christ's behalf; Be reconciled to GOD.

Romans 12:2 NIV

Do not conform to the pattern of this world, but be transformed by the renewing of your mind. Then you will be able to test and approve what GOD'S Will is — His Good, pleasing and Perfect Will. For The Cross makes us Clean. We are all flawed, but Christ Cleaned us up by His "Inside Job". He cleaned us up from the inside out. You, however, are not in the realm of the flesh but are in the realm of The Spirit, if indeed The Spirit of GOD lives in you. And if anyone does not have The Spirit of Christ, they do not belong to Christ. We appear before GOD washed Clean on Justice Day. And tribute Glory to GOD in every situation, for He is in each situation.

Church mandates to Preach Jesus.

John 3:16 (NIV) For GOD so Loved the world that He gave His One and Only Son, that whoever Believes in Him shall not perish but have Eternal Life.

Psalms 68:34-35 Reads (NIV):

Proclaim The Power of GOD, whose Majesty is over Israel, whose Power is in The Heavens. You, GOD, are awesome in your Sanctuary; The GOD of Israel gives Power and Strength to His people.

PRAISE BE TO GOD!!!

WALKING CLOSER WITH JESUS!!!

July 6, 2015

COLOSSIANS 3:16 (All NIV)
"LET CHRIST'S WORD DWELL IN YOU RICHLY!"
These are the five things we must do
to activate GOD'S Word:

1. READ GOD'S WORD - THE BIBLE. The more you read The Bible, the more we will learn of Christ Himself.

Hebrews 4:12-13 reads (NIV):

*** For The Word of GOD IS alive and active. Sharper than any double-edged sword, it penetrates even to dividing Soul and Spirit, joints and marrow; it judges the thoughts and attitudes of the heart; nothing in all creation is hidden from GOD'S sight. Everything is uncovered and; laid bare before the eyes of Him to Whom we must give account.

2. Meditate on and let the richness sink in and think about His Word often.

Psalms 119:108-109 and 112 NIV

*** Accept, LORD, the willing praise of my mouth, and Teach me Your Ways though constantly I take my Life in my hands, I will not forget Your Laws. My heart is set on keeping Your Decrees to the very end.

3. BELIEVE IT!!! Let go and let GOD in!!! Faith requires belief.

***Once when Jesus was Praying in private and His Disciples were with Him, He asked them, "Who do you say I am?" They replied, "Some say John The Baptist; others say Elijah; and still others, that one of the prophets of long ago has come back to Life. "But what about you?" He asked. "Who do you say I am?" Peter answered, "GOD'S Messiah."

4. LIVE IT!!! Our Daily Walk is a personal Relationship with our LORD, Jesus Christ!!!

5. WALK daily with Jesus!!! Let Him transform us to be His image!!! BE more Christ-like!!!

Romans 12:2 NIV

Do not conform to the pattern of this world, but be transformed by the renewing of your mind. Then you will be able to test and approve what God's Will is - His good, pleasing and perfect Will.

In Jesus Holy, Heavenly Name, we Pray!!! A-MEN!!!
Blessed be your days!!!

GOD IS LIFE!!!

May 18,2015
(All NIV)

*** The red of the bracelets stand for The Blood of Jesus washing our sins.

Read: 1 John 1:9

*** The white is our sins washed white as snow.

Read: Isaiah 1:18, Psalm 51:7

*** Place the bracelet on your right hand with the letters facing your fingers, so you can be a witness to others, who ask about the bracelet.

*** The purpose of the right hand is that it is the hand that GOD extends down to us to save us from our drowning world.

Read: Isaiah 41:10

So, as we usher out last year, we need to remember when we "ring in" the new year, not only to give thanks to GOD for The Blessings of last year, but the Blessings of the Future!!! If you are not already Saved, this is the Time to do it!!! Time awaits no one!!!

Romans 3:23-25 For all have sinned and fall short of the Glory of GOD and all are justified freely by His Grace through the Redemption that came by Christ Jesus. GOD presented Christ as a Sacrifice of Atonement, through the shedding of The Blood to be received by Faith.

Read: Psalm 4:4

BLESSED BE THE ONES WHO HEAR!!!
IN JESUS' HOLY NAME, WE PRAY!!! A-MEN!!!

For a suggested donation of $20.00, you can have your very own Bible and two bracelets; one bracelet for you, and one for you to share The Message with a Loved one!!! Be a witness for THE LORD!!! Let go and Let GOD!!!

For each donation received, a Bible and two bracelets will be sent, so that you, too, can Spread The Word of GOD!!!

SHARING IS CARING; CARE TO SHARE!!!

BOOKS OF THE BIBLE

Old Testament

Genesis
Exodus
Leviticus
Numbers
Deuteronomy
Joshua
Judges
Ruth
1 Samuel
2 Samuel
1 Kings
2 Kings
1Chronicles
2Chronicles Ezra
Nehemiah
Esther Job
Psalms
Proverbs
Ecclesiastes
Song of Songs

Isaiah
Jeremiah
Lamentations
Ezekiel
Daniel
Hosea
Joel
Amos
Obadiah
Jonah
Micah
Nahum
Habakkuk
Malachi

New Testament

Matthew
Mark
Luke
John
Acts

Romans
1Corinthians
2Corinthians
Galatians
Ephesians
Philippians
Colossians
1 Thessalonians
2 Thessalonians
1 Timothy
2 Timothy
Titus
Philemon
Hebrews
James
1 Peter
2 Peter
1 John
2 John
3 John
Jude
Revelation

Blessed is the one who reads and meditates on His Holy Word Daily...